Address all inquiries to:
Baobab Books
Email: bbfbooks@gmail.com
ISBN-13:
978-0-692528907 (Baobab Publishing)

Author's Bio

Schertevear Watkins is a former educator and divorced mother of two. Her love for teaching is her inspiration for writing Children's Literature. Schertevear's goal is to bring positive influences into the lives of as many children as possible through her characters. Schertevear writes books that promote learning, character development, social skills, family and more.

Author's Bio

Susieann Beavers-Harris is a former Pre-kindergarten transition coach and has volunteered in Pre-K classrooms. In the classroom, she saw the area's most challenging for early learners. Knowing that there are many children that need the extra preparation for elementary school, Susieann was inspired to contribute to this learning series.

LOOK OUT FOR THESE OTHER TITLES FROM

BLOOMING READERS

on

a and baobabpublishing.com

- Basic Sight Word Book
- Basic Sight Word: People, Places and Things Book
- Basic Sight Word: Action Word Book
- Basic Sight Word: Look, Taste. Feel, Smell and Sound Book
- Basic Sight Word: Pronoun Book
- Basic Sight Word: Careers Book

THIS BOOK BELONGS TO

This is **Mama, Daddy** and **me.**

Grandma and Suzy went to the store.

Grandpa is pulling Tim in the wagon.

Ray and his **friend** Joe walk to school.

My **name** is Nick.

Chad's **stepfather** is really cool.

This **brother** and **sister** are playing together.

I have a **twin** brother
named Rick.

Don's **stepmother** reads him a bedtime story.

Ben's **stepsister** Lena has lots of dolls.

Gabby's **stepbrother** is seven today.

Riya's dog Lulu is
her **pet.**

Amber and **Cousin** Pam
are sack racing.

Ruby's **godmother** took her to the park.

Jill and **Aunt** Mary bake a cake.

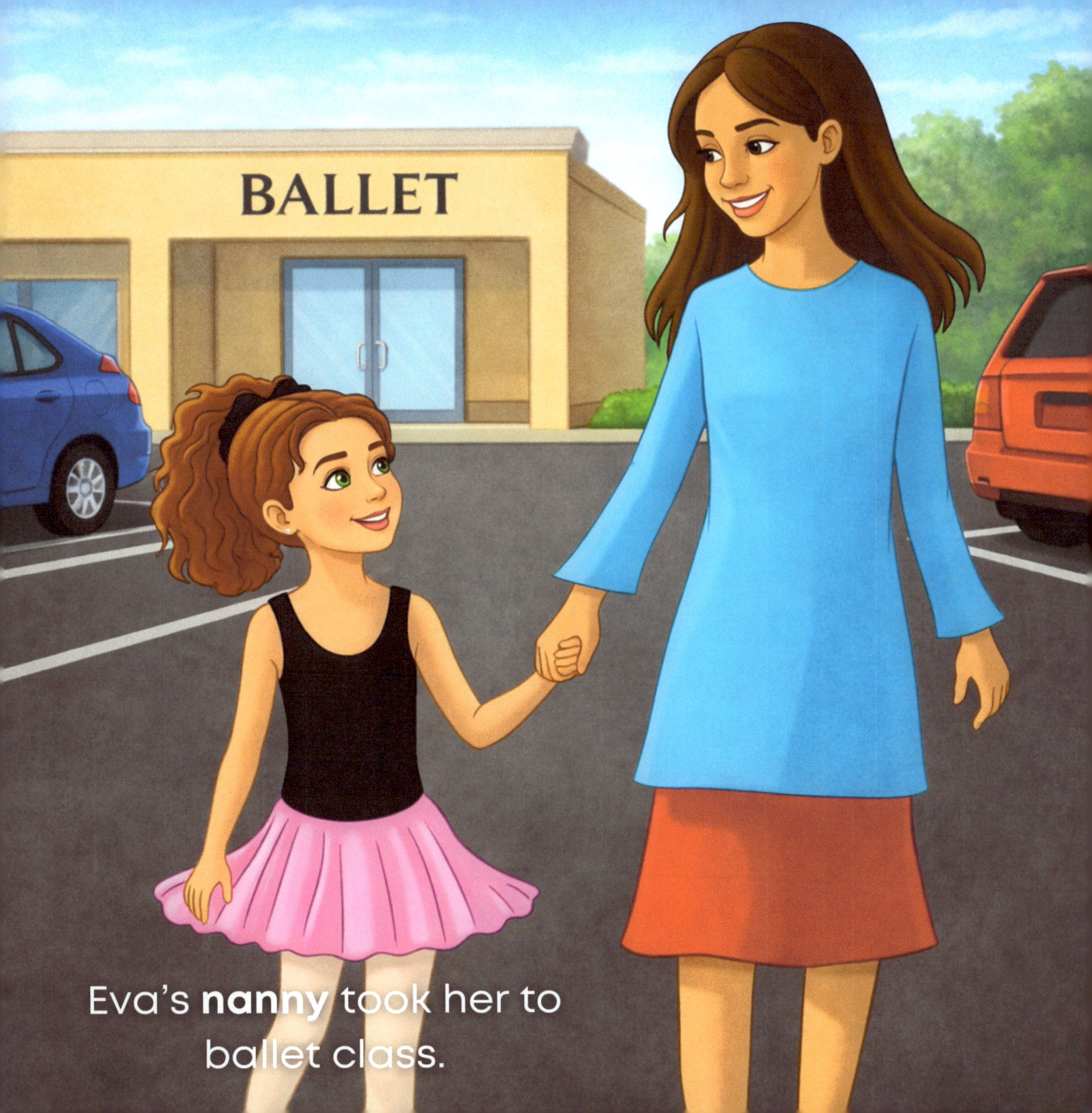

Eva's **nanny** took her to ballet class.

Amber and **Uncle** Joe are singing and dancing.

My **godfather** and I agree that families are cool.

ABOUT OUR LEARNING SYSTEM

BLOOMING READERS

Blooming readers is not just a random series of books. It is a unique Early Reading Tool that simultaneously introduces strategically selected high frequency words, and parts of speech.

Try playing sentence games by putting nouns, verbs, and adjectives together taught in our books. When books are purchased in order, our sight words can be combined to form hundreds of sentences.

MORE TO LEARN

Using The Book

Read this book with your early reader. Touch the words in bold as you read them. Ask your child to show you the character in the book that the word is referring to.
Make it fun and relatable. Ask questions as you read to your child. "What do you think about_?" or "Would you like __?" "Does your sister __?" or "Have you ever __?"
Reading Ready - When your child is ready, allow him/her to read to you. Starting out, alternate the pages. You may read all the pages on the left and he/she read the pages on the right.

Beyond The Book

To give your child more practice with the sight words introduced in this book, try making flash cards.
What you'll need-All you need is a black marker and blank index cards or sentence strips.
How to use- If your goal is to teach your child the words in this book, read the book at least twice a week with your child. Also, review the sight word flash cards with your child at least three times a week for about five minutes.
Something to Consider-No need for a picture. Letters are, in a sense pictures. Often times when children use illustrated flash cards they are looking at the picture and not the word. The picture becomes a distraction for some children.

WORD LIST

Parents	Stepmother	Grandpa
Uncle	Stepbrother	Aunt
Grandma	Cousin	Nanny
Mama	Stepfather	Daddy
Pet	Brother	Godmother
Sister	Godfather	Stepsister
Families	Twin	Friend

VISUAL OF HOW TO USE THE INDEX CARDS WITH THE WORDS FROM THIS SERIES

Follow the author.

www.ingramcontent.com/pod-product-compliance
Lightning Source LLC
LaVergne TN
LVHW070206110826
845147LV00002B/518

9780692528907